THE FOOTBALL JOKES AND QUIZ BOOK FOR KIDS

AWESOME FUN FOR SPORTS MAD KIDS

M. PREFONTAINE

CONTENTS

FOOTBALL JOKES

Q: Why did the goal post get angry?

A: Because the bar was rattled.

Q: What ship holds 20 football teams but only three leave it each season?

A: The Premier-ship

Q: What is a game of Football?

A: It has been described as a game with twenty-two players, two linesmen and 20,000 referees.

Q: How did the football pitch end up as triangle?

A: Somebody took a corner

Q: Why were the two managers sitting around sketching crockery before the start of the game?

A: It was a cup draw

Q: Why did the chicken get sent off?

A: For persistent fowl play

Q: Which insect didn't play well in goal?

A: The fumble bee

Q: **What do Manchester United and US Navy have in common?**

A: *They both spent 50mil on a sub.*

Q: **What is a ghosts favorite soccer position?**

A: *Ghoul keeper.*

Q: **Why did a footballer take a piece of rope onto the pitch?**

A: *He was the skipper*

Q: **What is a cheerleaders favourite colour?**

A: *Yeller*

Q: **How many Grimsby supporters does it take to change a light bulb?**

A: *Both of them*

Q: **Why do artists never win when they play football?**

A: *They keep drawing*

Q: **Why can't Cinderella play soccer?**

A: *Because she always runs away from the ball.*

Q: Which football side did Shy Barry and Very Quiet Vernon play for?

A: *The reserve-d team.*

Q: When is a footballer like a baby?

A: *When he dribbles*

Q: What runs along the edge of the pitch but never moves?

A: *The sideline*

Q: What kind of tea do soccer players drink?

A: *Penal-Tea*

Q: What do Lionel Messi and a magician have in common?

A: *Both do hat-tricks*

Q: When fish play football, who is the captain?

A: *The team's kipper*

Q: What happened when the pitch was flooded during a World Cup match?

A: *The teams brought on their subs.*

Q: What do you call someone who stands inside goalposts and stops the ball rolling away?

A: Annette

Q: What is the difference between Arsenal and a bra?

A: They both have lots of support but Arsenal have no cups.

Q: Which footballer makes the best coffee?

A: Diego Costa

Q: Why are scrambled eggs like a losing soccer team?

A: Because they've both been beaten.

Q: What do you call it when a dinosaur gets a goal?

A: dino-score

Q: Why didn't the skeleton play football?

A: His heart wasn't in it

Q: Where do a American players go when they need a new football shirt?

A: New Jersey.

Q: When should football players wear armour?

A: *When they play knight games.*

Q: What is harder to catch the faster you run?

A: *Your breath.*

Q: Why did the football quit the team?

A: *It was tired of being kicked around.*

Q: Why was Cinderella such a poor football player?

A: *Her coach was a pumpkin.*

Q: Why is it always warmer after a football game?

A: *All the fans have left.*

Q: What's the difference between a battery and Inter Milan?

A: *A battery has a positive side*

Q: What is black and white and black and white and black and white ?

A: *A Newcastle fan rolling down a hill*

Q: Which football team loves ice-cream?

A: *Aston Vanilla*

Q: What's the difference between The Invisible Man and Scotland?

A: *You've got more chance of seeing The Invisible Man at the World Cup Finals*

Q: What's the difference between Scotland and a tea bag?

A: *The tea bag stays in the cup longer.*

Q: Why shouldn't you play soccer in the jungle?

A: *There are too many cheetahs*

Q: How do soccer players stay cool during games?

A: *They stand near the fans.*

Q: Why was the best footballer in the world asked to tidy up their room?

A: *Because they were Messi.*

Q: What part of a football pitch smells nicest?

A: *The scenter spot*

Q: What is the bank manager's favourite type of football?

A: Fiver side.

Q. What runs around a soccer field but never moves?

A: A fence

Q: Which team is the chewiest?

A: The Toffees

Q: How do birds cheer for their soccer teams?

A: They egg them on.

Q: Why did the chicken get ejected from the soccer game?

A: For persistent fowl play.

Q: How do you stop squirrels playing football in the garden?

A: Hide the ball, it drives them nuts.

Q: Why do managers bring suitcases along to away games?

A: So that they can pack the defense.

Q: If you have a referee in football, what do you have in bowls?

A: *Cornflakes*

Q: **What's the chilliest ground in the premiership?**

A: *Cold Trafford*

Q: **Why didn't the dog want to play soccer?**

A: *He was a boxer.*

Q: **Why was the soccer field wet on a sunny day?**

A: *The players dribbled all over it.*

Q: **What does a Tottenham fan do after watching their team win the Premier League?**

A: *Turn off the PlayStation*

Q: **Which soccer player keeps the field neat?**

A: The sweeper.

Q: **Why don't they drink tea at Emirates Stadium?**

A: *Because all the cups are in Manchester.*

Q: **Why don't grasshoppers play football?**

A: *They prefer cricket*

Q: **Why did the manager bring pencils and a sketchbook to the team meeting?**

A: He was hoping to get a draw.

Q: Who scored the most goals in the fictional animals' game?
A: The Centaur Forward

Q: What do you get if you cross a football team and a wood?

A: Nottingham Forest

Q: Why wasn't the nose on the soccer team?

A: It didn't get picked.

Q: What time is it when an elephant steps on your soccer ball?

A: Time to get a new ball

Q: What's the difference between the Prince of Wales and a throw in?

A: One is heir to the throne, the other is thrown in the air

Q: Where do football directors go when they are fed up?

A: The bored room.

Q: What part of a football ground is never the same?

A: The changing rooms

Q: What is a goal keepers favourite snack?

A: Beans on post

Q: Why did the footballer hold his boot to his ear?

A: Because he liked sole music

Q: What did the Llama say when he was kicked out of the team?

A: Alpaca my bags

Q: What is a Cheerleader's favorite food?

A: Cheerios

Q: How many Liverpool fans does it take to change a light bulb?

A: None they just sit around talking about how good the old one was.

Q: What gave the centre forward the power to walk through the wall?

A: A door

Q: What football club do sheep like?

A: Baaaaaaaaa-rcelona.

Q: Why are the dirty kids so good at soccer?

A: *Because they are Messi.*

Q: Why are soccer players excellent at math?

A: *They know how to use their heads.*

Q: What do you call 23 millionaires around a TV watching the World Cup final?

A: *The England national team.*

Q: What's the difference between Rangers and a Student Rail Card?

A: *With a Student Rail Card you get four weeks in Europe.*

Q. If David Beckham were to become one of the Spice Girls which one would he turnout to be?

A: *Waste of Spice*

Q: Why was the tiny ghost asked to join the football team?

A: *They needed a little team spirit.*

Q: What do you call a Scottish player in the first round of the World Cup?

A: *The Referee.*

Q: Why aren't the England football team allowed to own a dog?

A: Because they can't hold on to a lead.

Q: How many Manchester City soccer fans does it take to change a lightbulb?

A: None - they're quite happy living in the shadows.

Q. What's the difference between a Hibernian fan and a coconut?

A. You can get a drink out of a coconut.

Q: What's the difference between a PG Tips monkey and a Scottish footballer?

A: A PG Tips monkey has been seen holding a cup.

Q: What do you call a Chelsea fan on the moon?

A: A Problem.

Q: What do you call all the Chelsea fans on the moon?

A: Problem solved

FUNNY STORIES

During the World Cup in Brazil, the England team visited an orphanage. "It was heart-breaking to see their sad little faces with no hope," said João, age 6.

As the Ranger's struggles continued, a pound coin was thrown onto the pitch. Police are trying to determine whether it was a missile or a takeover bid.

God and the devil were having an argument, and Satan proposed a football game between heaven and hell to resolve the dispute. God, in his eternal goodness, pointed out that it wouldn't be a fair match because all the 'good' players go to heaven. The devil smiled, replying, "Yes, but we've got all the refs.

Rafael Benitez was wheeling his shopping trolley across the supermarket car park when he noticed an old lady struggling with her shopping. He stopped and asked, "Can you manage dear?" to which the old lady replied, "no way you got yourself into this mess, don't ask me to sort it out."

A team of mammals were playing a team of insects. The mammals totally dominated the first half and at half-time were leading 39-nil. However, at half-time the insects made a substitution and brought on a centipede.

The centipede scored no less than 180 goals and the insects won the game by miles. In the dressing room afterwards the captain of the mammals was chatting to the insect captain.

"That centipede of yours is terrific," the captain of the mammals said. "Why didn't you play him from the start?"

"We'd have liked to," replied the insect captain, "but it takes him 45 minutes to get his boots on."

A match between two non-League teams took place last winter in the North of England. It had been raining heavily all week and the ground resembled a swamp.

However, the referee ruled that play was possible and tossed the coin to determine ends.

The visiting captain won the toss and, after a moment's thought, said, 'OK - we'll take the shallow end.'

'We're starting up an amateur football team. Would you care to join?'

'I would, yes, but I'm afraid I don't know, the first thing about football.'

'That's all right. We need a referee as well.'

Our club manager won't stand for any nonsense. Last Saturday he caught a couple of fans climbing over the stadium wall.

He was furious. He grabbed them by the collars and said,

"Now you just get back in there and watch the game till it finishes."

A rather dim fan arrives at a football match midway through the second half.

"What's the score?" he asks his friend as he settles into his seat.

"Nil-nil," comes the reply.

"And what was the score at half-time?" he asks.

A football hooligan appeared in court charged with disorderly conduct and assault. The arresting officer, giving evidence, stated that the accused had thrown something into the canal. `What exactly was it that he threw into the canal' asked the magistrate.

'Stones, sir.'

'Well, that's hardly an offence is it' said the magistrate?'

'It was in this case, sir,' said the police officer. 'Stones was the referee.'

Three fans were bemoaning the fact that their team kept losing and was facing relegation.

"I blame the manager" said the first, "if he would sign new players then we could be a great side"

"I blame the players" said the second, "if they made more effort I am sure we would score more goals"

"I blame my parents", added the third, " if I'd been born in another town I'd be supporting a decent team.

After a visit to the doctor, Joe Bloggs, the city team's centre forward dropped in to his local pub for a quick one. "What's up mate?" asked his friend Brian, "you look worried."

"Yes, I am," Joe replied. "I've just been to the doctor's and he told me I can't play football."

"Oh, really?" said Brian. "He's seen you play too then, has he?"

A rather dim fan arrives at a football match midway through the second half.

It was mid-way through the football season and a third division team were doing really badly. The manager decided to get the team together and go back to absolute basics. Picking up a football, he said,

"Right, lads, what I have in my hands is called a football, and the object of the game is..."

"Hang on a minute," came a shout, "you're going too fast."

Striker: "I had an open goal but still I didn't score. I could kick myself."

Manager: "I wouldn't bother. You'd probably miss."

It's a funny old game, football,' as the captain said to the manager after his team had been trounced 6-0 in an important relegation match.

To which the manager replied grimly, 'Yes - but it isn't meant to be.

Football has been described as a game with twenty-two players, two linesmen and 20,000 referees.

A young autograph hunter was really chuffed when he got Jordan Henderson's autograph after a match.

The following week he accosted Henderson's once more and got his autograph, and after the next game he tried to get it yet again.

"Look here," said Henderson, "this is the third time you've asked for my autograph. What's going on?"

"Well," said the young man, "if I can get eight more of yours, I can swap them for one of Salah's."

Ref:I'm sending you off

Player: What for?

Ref: The rest of the match.

Manager: Twenty teams in the league and you lot finish bottom?

Captain: Well, it could have been worse.

Manager: How?

Captain: There could have been more teams in the league

Paul took his seat in the 3rd row of the stadium for the big football match.

Upon looking around, he was surprised to see his young neighbor, James, in the front row.

"Hi, James" He called out.

James turned around. "Hi, Paul" he called back.

"How did you get the front row ticket?" Paul asked.

James answered, "From my older brother."

Paul asked, "Where is he?"

James answered, "At home looking for his ticket"

Two football fans are walking along the road when one of them picks up a mirror. He looks in it and says,

'Hey, I know that bloke!'

The second one picks it up and says,

'Of course, you do you idiot, it's me'.

'now White arrived home one evening to find her home destroyed by fire. She was especially worried because she'd left all seven dwarves asleep inside.

As she scrambled among the wreckage, frantically calling their names, suddenly she heard the cry, 'Portsmouth for the Cup.'

'Thank goodness,' sobbed Snow White. 'At least Dopey is still alive'.

I met a fairy today who said she would grant me one wish.

"I want to live forever," I said.

"Sorry," said the fairy, "but I am not allowed to grant that type of wish."

"Fine," I said, "then I want to die when England next win the World Cup."

"You crafty devil!" said the fairy.

An Aston Villa fan walks into a pub with his dog just as the football scores come on the TV. The announcer says that Aston Villa have lost 3-0 and the dog immediately rolls over on its back, sticks its paws in the air and plays dead.

"That's amazing," says the barman, "what does he do when they win?"

The Aston Villa Fan scratches his head for a couple of minutes and finally replies, "I dunno... I've only had the dog for eight months."

I was playing Football Manager on my PC when I was offered the Scotland job. I knew it was a poor squad with no future, so I declined the offer. I then put the phone down and got back to Football Manager.

Two blokes were walking through a cemetery when they happened upon a tombstone that read:

"Here lies John White, a good man and a Chelsea fan."

So, one of them asked the other: "When the hell did they start putting two people in one grave?"

Interviewer: **Who is the best striker in the premier league.**

Ibrahimovic: **For me I like a striker that makes the difference.**

Lukaku is strong, he's more the physical player that scores a lot of goals. Aguero, he's good.

Interviewer: **You din't said yourself , I was expecting you to say 'Me'.**

Ibrahimovic: **Lions. they don't compare themselves with humans.**

FUNNY FOOTBALL QUOTES

And with 4 minutes gone, the score is already 0-0.
Ian Dark

Sandro's holding his face. You can tell from that it's a knee injury.
Dion Dublin

I'm going to make a prediction - it could go either way.
Ron Atkinson

Strangely, in slow motion replay, the ball seemed to hang in the air for even longer. *David Acfield*

Who'll win the league? It's a toss of a coin between three of them.
Matt le Tissier

For those of you watching in black and white, Spurs are in the all-yellow strip.
John Motson

He dribbles a lot and the opposition don't like it - you can see it all over their faces.
Ron Atkinson

I never make predictions, and I never will.
Paul Gascoigne

I always used to put my right boot on first, and then obviously my right sock.
Barry Venison

My parents have been there for me, ever since I was about 7.
David Beckham

If Everton were playing at the bottom of the garden, I'd pull the curtains.
Bill Shankley

I would not be bothered if we lost every game as long as we won the league.
Mark Viduka

The best side drew.
BillShankley

Without being too harsh on David Beckham, he cost us the match.
Ian Wright

The first ninety minutes of a football match are the most important.
Sir Bobby Robson

Like and Egyptian fish he is living in denial.
James Richardson

Roma and Lazio, like Penelope Pitstop, are tied on points.
James Richardson

It's end to end stuff, but from side to side. *Trevor Brooking*

When you are 4-0 up you should never lose 7-1.
Lawrie Mcmenemy.

I wouldn't say I was the best manager in the business. But I was in the top one.
Brian Clough

Well Kerry, you're 19 and you're a lot older than a lot of people younger than yourself. *Mike Gray.*

Wilkins sends an inch perfect pass to no one in particular.
Byron Butler.

Allegations are all very well but I would like to know who these alligators are.
Ron Saunders

I came to Nantes two years ago and it's much the same today, except that it's totally different.
Kevin Keegan

Celtic manager Davie Hay still has a fresh pair of legs up his sleeve.
John Greig

That was only a yard away from being an inch-perfect pass.
Murdo Macleod.

Hearts are now playing with a five-man back four.
Alan McInally

Solskjaer never misses the target. That time he hit the post.
Peter Schmeichel

Beckham? His wife can't sing and his barber can't cut hair.
Brian Clough

He's got a knock on his shin there, just above the knee.
Frank Stapleton

I was surprised, but I always say nothing surprises me in football.
Les Ferdinand.

It was like the ref had a brand new yellow card and wanted to see if it worked.
Richard Rufus.

As with every young player, he's only 18.
Alex Ferguson

As long as no one scored, it was always going to be close.
Arsene Wenger

We lost because we didn't win.
Ronaldo

That would've been a goal had it gone inside the post.
Michael Owen

I'm not saying he's pale and thin, but the maid in our hotel room pulled back the sheets and remade the bed without realising he was still in it.
Brian Clough

When they don't score, they hardly ever win. *Michael Owen*

I've been consistent in patches this season.
Theo Walcott

Giroud scored a brilliant header with the last kick of the game.
Chris Kamara

If you're not sure what to do with the ball, just pop it in the net and we'll discuss your options afterwards.
Bill Shankley

It's real end-to-end stuff, but unfortunately, it's all up at Forest's end.
Chris Kamara

Jordan Henderson is a player who likes to do his business in the middle of the park.
Jason McAteer

Mind you, I've been here during the bad times too - one year we came second.
Bob Paisley

In his interviews, Beckham manages to sit on the fence very well and keeps both ears on the ground.
Brian Kerr

At Liverpool we always said we had the best two teams on Merseyside, Liverpool and Liverpool Reserves.
Bill Shankley

If we can play like that every week, we'll get some level of consistency.
Alex Ferguson

We didn't underestimate them but they were a lot better than we thought.
Bobby Robson

Please don't call me arrogant, but I'm European champion and I think I'm a special one
Jose Mourinho

Andy Ritchie has now scored 11 goals, exactly double the number he scored last season.
Alan Parry

If that had gone in it would have been a goal. *David Coleman*

Don't tell those coming in now the result of that fantastic match. Now let's have another look at Italy's winning goal.
David Coleman

England don't have to score tonight, but they do have to win.
Billy McNeill

I am a firm believer that if you score one goal the other team have to score two to win. *Howard Wilkinson*

Alex Ferguson is the best manager I've ever had at this level. Well, he's the only manager I've actually

had at this level. But he's the best manager I've ever had.
David Beckham

If you don't believe you can win, there is no point in getting out of bed at the end of the day.
Neville Southall

I've had 14 bookings this season – 8 of which were my fault, but 7 of which were disputable.
Paul Gascoigne

I've never wanted to leave. I'm here for the rest of my life, and hopefully after that as well.
Alan Shearer

I'd like to play for an Italian club, like Barcelona.
Mark Draper

You've got to believe that you're going to win, and I believe we'll win the World Cup until the final whistle blows and we're knocked out.
Peter Shilton

I faxed a transfer request to the club at the beginning of the week but let me state that I don't want to leave Leicester.
Stan Collymore

I was watching the Blackburn game on TV on Sunday when it flashed on the screen that George (Ndah) had scored in the first minute at Birmingham. My first reaction was to ring him up. Then I remembered he was out there playing.

Ade Akinbiyi

I'm as happy as I can be – but I have been happier.
Ugo Ehiogu

Leeds is a great club and it's been my home for years, even though I live in Middleborough.
Jonathan Woodgate

I can see the carrot at the end of the tunnel.
Stuart Pearce

I took a whack on my left ankle, but something told me it was my right.
Lee Hendrie

I couldn't settle in Italy – it was like living in a foreign country.
Ian Rush

Germany are a very difficult team to play...they had 11 internationals out there today.
Steve Lomas

The Brazilians were South American, and the Ukrainians will be more European.
Phil Neville

All that remains is for a few dots and commas to be crossed.
Mitchell Thomas

One accusation you can't throw at me is that I've always done my best.
Alan Shearer

I'd rather play in front of a full house than an empty crowd.
Johnny Giles

We must have had 99 percent of the game. It was the other three percent that cost us the match.
Ruud Gullit

The beauty of Cup football is that Jack always has a chance of beating Goliath.
Terry Butcher.

There is no in between – you're either good or bad. We were in between.
Gary Lineker.

Some people believe football is a matter of life and death. I'm very disappointed with that attitude. I can assure you it is much, much more important than that.
Bill Shankly

You can't say my team aren't winners. They've proved that by finishing fourth, third and second in the last three years.
Gerard Houllier

Football is a simple game; 22 men chase a ball for 90 minutes and at the end, the Germans win.
Gary Lineker

SPORTS ONE LINERS

named my dog 6 miles so I can tell people that I walk 6 miles every single day.

7 days without soccer makes one weak

I like to think outside the box, which has rather hindered my goalkeeping career.

The other day, I went to KFC. I didn't know Kentucky had a football club.

Just burned 2,000 calories. That's the last time I leave brownies in the oven while I nap.

Today a man knocked on my door and asked for a small donation towards the local swimming pool. I gave him a glass of water.

The depressing thing about tennis is that no matter how good I get, I'll never be as good as a wall.

They used to time me with a stopwatch... now they use a calendar.

My tennis opponent was not happy with my serve. He kept returning it.

The skydiving club disbanded because they had a falling out.

Some flies were playing football in a saucer, using a sugar lump as a ball. One of them said, "We'll have to do better than this, lads. We're playing in the cup tomorrow."

The World Cup Final is the same day as Amazon Prime Day, so if it is coming home it'll get here incredibly quickly.

A burglary was recently committed at West Ham's ground, and the entire contents of the trophy room were stolen. The London police are looking for a man with a claret & blue carpet.

Apparently, the England FA is under investigation by the HMRC for tax evasion. Word is Lancaster Gate have been claiming for Silver Polish for the past 48 years.

Everton have a new sponsor - Easy Jet. In and Out of Europe in 90 minutes.

Oxo were going to bring out a Euro 2020 Commemorative cube painted red, white and blue in honour of the England squad. But it was a laughing stock and crumbled in the box.

FOOTBALL LIMERICKS

Was it City, United or Town

Got promoted and then went back down?

It was one of the three,

But it mystifies me,

Which is why I walk round with a frown.

There was a goalkeeper called Walter,

Who played on the island of Malta,

But his kicks were so long,

And the wind was so strong,

That the ball ended up in Gibraltar

There was a young striker from Spain

Who hated to play in the rain.

One day in a muddle

He stepped in a puddle

And got washed away in a drain.

There was a young player from Clyde,

Took a penalty kick that went wide,

That next match his brother,

Well, he missed another,

And now neither can get in the side!

A striker from somewhere in Kent,

Took free kicks which dipped and then bent,

In a match on the telly ,

He gave one some welly ,

And the keeper the wrong way he sent.

There was a young striker from Reading

Who bumped his brow on a door at a wedding.

It made his head swell

But he said `Just as well,

'Cos now I'll improve on my heading.'

A player who turned out for Dover,

Had no shirt, so he wore a pullover,

But the thing was too long,

And he put it on wrong,

So that all he could do was fall over

A striker who came from Devizes,

Did little to help to win prizes,

When asked for a reason,

He said, 'Well, this season,

My boots were of two different sizes!'

A footballer in from the States

Was paid at very high rates.

But when he lost touch

He wasn't worth much.

Now he just kicks around with his mates.

The wonderful Wizard of Oz

Retired from football because,

When he tried to run fast

His legs didn't last

'Cos he wasn't the wizard he was.

There was a young player from Tottenham,

His manners he'd gone and forgotten 'em.

One day at the doc's

He took off his socks,

Because he complained he felt hot in 'em.

Little Jack Horner once took a corner,

And belted the ball so high,

With the keeper upset,

It went straight in the net,

So he said, 'What a good boy am I'.

A team of footballers from Stroud,

Had supporters who shouted too loud,

When all ceased their din,

Goals just rocketed in,

So now they're a much quieter crowd.

There was a young player called Kelly,

Who couldn't play 'cos of his belly,

When he ran on the pitch,

He caused a big ditch,

So he just watches games on the telly.

DID YOU KNOW?

Fun facts about the Premier League.

1. Only two players have scored penalties with both feet in the Premier League – Bobby Zamora and Obafemi Martins

2. In 2014/15 Leicester spent 140 days at the bottom of the table, more than any other team without being relegated. They won the League the following season at odds of 5,000 to 1.

3. Mario Balotelli only made one assist in the Premier League. It was to Sergio Aguerra against QPR to win the title.

4. Paul Robinson, the former England goalkeeper has more Premier League assists than any other keeper (5). He has also scored and won a penalty.

5. The goalkeeper Richard Wright has played 12 Premier League games, Arsenal (12) and Man City (0), and has two Premier League medals.

6. Alan Shearer has missed the most Premier League penalties (11). He has scored the most though (56)

7. Richard Dunne (Manchester City, Aston Villa & Queens Park Rangers; 2004/05 - 2014/15) has scored the most Premier League own goals (10).

8. Ryan Giggs has 13 Premier League winners medals.

9. Marcus Bent has played for a record 8 Premier League clubs - (Crystal Palace, Blackburn Rovers, Ipswich Town, Leicester City, Everton, Charlton Athletic, Wigan Athletic & Wolverhampton Wanderers; 1997/98 - 2010/11)

10. Gareth Bale is the only player to score, get an assist, get booked and score an own goal in a single EPL match, against Liverpool on Nov 28, 2012.

11. Chelsea fielded the league's first completely non-English starting line-up on Dec 26, 1999 against Southampton. They won 2-1.

12. No English manager has ever won the league title.

13. Ryan Giggs' dad played rugby for Wales.

14. Sir Alex Ferguson won 12 Premier League titles

15. Blackburn lead the red card charts with an amazing 75 red cards

16. Ledley King scored fastest goal after just 10 seconds against Bradford in 2000.

17. The highest attendance was 76,398 for Man Utd vs. Blackburn in 2007

18. The lowest attendance was 3,039 for Wimbledon vs. Everton 1993

19. Zlatan Ibrahimovic has played for six clubs that have won the Champions League, but he has never actually won the trophy himself

20. Norwich finished third in the 1992/1993 Premier League season, but had a goal difference of -4 after 42 games.

21. While she was managing director at Birmingham City, Karren Brady sold her husband Paul Peschisolido to Stoke for £400k in 1994. They got married a year later.

22. David Beckham and David Moyes played together at Preston North End.

23. Arsene Wenger has an asteroid named after him. It is called 33179 Arsènewenger

24. Dennis Bergkamp had a fear of flying, and has previously stated that he would rather miss European and World Cup matches with Arsenal and the Netherlands rather than fly to them.

25. Jack Rodwell went three years, eight months and 29 days without winning a Premier League match in which he started — a winless run of 39 games. It ended when Sunderland beat Crystal Palace 4 - 0.

PREMIER LEAGUE QUIZ

Some really tough Premier League questions to test the depth of your knowledge about the best league in the world.

You can try them out to see how much your family and friends know.

1. When was the Premier League founded?

2. How many teams competed in the first year?

3. Who were the first Premier League Champions?

4. Who is the leading goal scorer in the Premier League?

5. How many goals has he scored?

6. There are six teams who have been ever present in the PL since its formation. Who are they?

7. Which player has made the most consecutive PL appearances?

8. Which player has played for the most PL clubs?

9. What is Arsenal's ground called?

10. Which player has scored the most PL hat tricks and how many?

11. Five players have scored five goals in a single PL match. Who are they?

12. Which manager has managed the most PL clubs?

13. How many players were there not from the British Isles on the first day of the PL in 1992/93?

14. Who is the only player to have scored goals for 7 clubs in the PL?

15. How many London based teams were in the inaugural PL?

16. Who were the Premier League's first ever sponsors?

17. Which team was first to score 1000 home goals?

18. Who were the first team to concede 100 goals in a season?

19. Which Premier League Team's name starts with five consonants?

20. In August 1995 Alan Hansen said that 'you can't win anything with kids. Which team was he talking about?

21. Who scored a hat trick on 26th May 2006 in the last game at Highbury for Arsenal?

22. Who did Arsenal play in the last Highbury game.

23. Which is the only team to have played in the Premier League, the old Divisions 1, 2, 3 and 4, and Divisions 3 South and 3 North?

24. How many PL goals did Michael Owen score?

25. Who was nicknamed 'The Baby Faced Assassin'?

26. Who is the Algerian who has won the PFA Player of the Year?

27. Which team holds the record for the number of wins in a season?

28. If points and goal difference are equal between two or more teams, what is the third and final statistic used when ranking teams in the Premier League table?

29. Where was the first ever Premier League match outside England played?

30. What year did Arsene Wenger become manager of Arsenal?

31. In which season did Arsenal's 'Invincibles' remain unbeaten?

32. Which team eventually beat them?

33. Who was Arsenal's manager when the Premier League was founded in 1992?

34. Who is the Bournemouth Manager?

35. How many teams are currently in the Premier League?

36. Blackpool were in the Premier League for one season, which one?

37. Former Aston Villa striker Dwight Yorke represented which country?

38. Which Villa goalkeeper became the first to score in the Premier League?

39. Which Villa player won the Writers Association Players Player of the Year in the inaugural PL season?

40. What nationality is former Villa keeper Mark Bosnich?

41. What is Barnsley's nickname?

42. How many seasons have Barnsley been in the Premier League?

43. Who was their leading goal scorer in that season?

44. How many goals did they concede during this season?

45. What is Birmingham's ground called?

46. Which season did they achieve their highest PL finishing position?

47. Who was their top scorer that year?

48. Who is the all-time leading Premier League goal scorer for Birmingham?

49. What nationality is he?

50. Which year did Blackburn win the Premier League?

51. Who was their leading scorer?

52. Which Blackburn player scored the 5,000th PL goal on 7th December 1996?

53. What has been Blackburn's lowest position since they left the Premier League?

54. How much did Blackburn pay for Alan Shearer and who did they buy him from?

55. What is Bolton's nickname

56. How many seasons have Bolton been in the PL?

57. What has been their highest finishing PL position?

58. What is the Bolton ground called?

59. Who is the leading Premier League goal scorer for Bolton?

60. What is Bournemouth's mascot called?

61. What is Bournemouth's ground called?
62. How many people can it hold?

63. Which other club has Bournemouth manager Eddie How managed?

64. Which former Bournemouth player, who scored their winner against Grimsby to preserve their status in the Football League in 2009, has a stand named after him at their ground?

65. How many seasons have Bradford spent in the Premier League?

66. Who is the leading Premier League goal scorer for Bradford?

67. Who scored the first Premier League hat trick for Bradford City?

68. What is Bradford's ground called?

69. What did Rodney Marsh say he would do if Bradford City avoided relegation in the 1999-00 season?

70. Which German midfielder scored Brighton & Hove Albion's first goal in the Premier League in their 3-1 home win over West Brom in 2017?

71. Who is the leading PL goal scorer for Brighton?

72. What is Brighton's ground called?

73. What is Brighton's nickname?

74. Burnley holds the record for the most away losses in a season. How many and when?

75. Cardiff have played two seasons in the Premier League. Which one's?

76. Which year was Charlton's first year in the Premier League?

77. Who was their manager during this season?

78. Who is the Chelsea Owner?

79. Who is the leading Premier League goal scorer for Chelsea?

80. Who won the Golden Boot playing for Chelsea in 2000/01?

81. How many PL goals did Drogba score?

82. Which Chelsea footballer played every minute of the season for the club when they won the domestic league in 2017?

83. How many times have Chelsea won the PL?

84. How many seasons have Coventry spent in the PL?

85. Who is the leading PL goal scorer for Coventry?

86. Which Coventry player jointly won the Golden Boot in 1997/98?

87. Which Coventry player was the first African to play in the PL?

88. What is Coventry's ground called?

89. Coventry were a founding member of the PL in 1992/93. Who was their leading goal scorer that season?

90. What was Coventry's lowest league position since leaving the PL?

91. In 1992/93 Palace achieved the highest amount of points by a PL club that was relegated. How many points did they get?

92. Who is the leading PL goal scorer for Palace?

93. How many seasons have Palace been in the PL?

94. What is Crystal Palace's ground called?

95. Who was the manager before Roy Hodgson who was sacked after 77 days?

96. In 2007/08 Derby achieved the unwanted record of most Premier League games without a win. How many games?

97. Another unwanted record in 2007/08 was that they hold the record for the fewest goals in a PL season. How many did they get?

98. Yet another unwanted record was the record negative goal difference in the PL. How many?

99. Who is the leading PL goal scorer for Derby?

100. Derby holds the joint record for the most losses in a PL season. How many?

101. How many seasons were Derby in the PL?

102. What has been their highest PL finishing position?

103. Who is the only player to play in a Merseyside and a Glasgow derby?

104. On the 10th April 2005 a player scored for Everton and became the youngest ever scorer of a PL goal. Who was he and how old?

105. Which Everton player holds the joint record of 8 PL red cards?

106. Which Spanish coach took charge of Everton between June 2013 and May 2016?

107. Who was the centre back that Everton sold to Arsenal for £2m in February 1993?

108. What is Wayne Rooney's middle name?

109. What is Fulham's ground called?

110. Which musician's statue did Fulham have at their ground till it was moved to the National football Museum in 2014?

111. Which Fulham player scored the 15,000th goal in the PL on 30th December 2006?

112. Who is the leading PL goal scorer for Fulham?

113. What is the name of Huddersfields ground?

114. What Huddersfield's nickname?

115. When was Huddersfield's first season in the Premier League?

116. Who is the leading PL goal scorer for Hull?

117. How many seasons have Hull been in the PL?

118. In December 2008 Hull found themselves 4-0 down at Man City at half time. What did manager Phil Brown do?

119. What is Hull City's ground call?

120. What colour shirts do Hull Have?

121. How many seasons have Ipswich been in the Premier League?

122. On the 4th March 1995 Ipswich suffered the biggest away loss. Who was it against and what was the score?

123. Who is the leading PL goal scorer for Ipswich?

124. Who scored the first PL hat trick for Ipswich?

125. Ipswich holds the joint record for the most losses in a PL season. How many?

126. Which Leeds player scored the first PL hat trick?

127. Who is the leading PL goal scorer for Leeds?

128. Which Leeds player is the only person born before 1960 to score a PL hat trick?

129. Which Leeds player is the second youngest to score a PL goal?

130. Which Leeds player jointly won the Golden Boot in 1998/99?

131. Which Leicester player holds the record for scoring in the most goals in consecutive games?

132. Which Leicester player holds the joint record of 14 yellow cards in a season?

133. Who is the leading PL goal scorer for Leicester?

134. How many PL goals did Jaime Vardy score when Leicester won the title?

135. Who was the outfield player who played every minute of their title winning season?

136. What were the much quoted odds against Leicester winning the PL in the 20015/16 season?

137. What is Leicester's ground called?

138. Which Leicester player won the PFA Player of the Year for 2015/16?

139. Who is the leading PL goal scorer for Liverpool?

140. Who scored the first PL hat trick for Liverpool?

141. Who was Liverpool's first Premier League goalkeeper?

142. Who won the Golden Boot for Liverpool in 2013/14?

143. How many PL goals did Steven Gerrard score?

144. Jamie Carragher made his first team debut for Liverpool under which manager?

145. Which Chelsea defender did Luis Suarez bite in 2013?

146. Against which team did Steven Gerrard's slip happen in April 2014 which arguably cost Liverpool the title?

147. Who became the first African to score over 30 goals in a season for Liverpool?

148. Which Liverpool player won the PFA Player of the Year for 2005/06?

149. How many times have Liverpool won the PL?

150. Who did Liverpool sell Fernando Torres to?

151. How much was he sold for?

152. Who sued Man City after being sacked after being relegated in 2000-01?

153. In 2011/12 Man City won the Premier League by the smallest margin. What was the margin?

154. In 2006/07 Man City scored the record lowest number of home goals in a season. How many?

155. Man City played the oldest player to play PL. Who was it and what age was he?

156. Who is the leading PL goal scorer for Man City?

157. Who scored the first PL hat trick for Man City?

158. Who won the Golden Boot playing for Man City in 2010/11?

159. What was unusual about the Man City v Everton PL game on October 2nd 2005?

160. Who were Man City playing against on May 13th 2012 when they scored two injury time goals to secure the title?

161. Who scored the dramatic last goal in this game?

162. Which Man City goalkeeper holds the PL record for the longest drop kick?

163. In 2017/18 Man City set the record points total for the PL. How many?

164. What was their total PL goals in this season?

165. How many consecutive wins did Man City achieve in a PL record run in 2017/18?

166. In March 2018 Man City won 1-0 against Chelsea and set a record for the number of passes in a match. How many?

167. Who did Man City buy Kevin de Bruyne from?

168. Who did they buy Bernardo Silva from?

169. Which Man Utd player has played the most PL seasons?

170. Man Utd won the premier league by a record number of points at the time, beaten by Man City in 1917 - 18. How many and when?

171. Man Utd have the most Premier League titles. How many?

172. In 1993/94 Man Utd conceded the smallest number of home goals in a season. How many?

173. In 2011/12 Man Utd achieved the most points in the PL without actually winning the title. How many did they get and who beat them?

174. In 1996/97 they also achieved the fewest points to win the title. How many points did they get?

175. A Man Utd player has scored the most PL goals for a single club. Who is it and how many did he score?

176. Which Man Utd player holds the record for the number of PL assists?

177. Which Man Utd goalkeeper went a record 14 consecutive PL games without conceding a goal?

178. How many PL titles did Sir Alex Ferguson win?

179. How many Manager of the Season awards did Sir Alex win?

180. Sir Alex Ferguson holds the record for the most PL wins. How many did he achieve?

181. Which Man Utd player won the Golden Boot in 2002/03?

182. How many PL goals did Ryan Giggs score?

183. What are David Beckham's two middle names?

184. Which Man Utd player was the first player to score five goals in a match?

185. Who played every minute of United's title winning season of 1992/93?

186. Who were United playing when Eric Cantona performed his infamous 'Kung Fu kick'?

187. On the 12th February 2011 Wayne Rooney scored famously a winning goal with an overhead bicycle kick. Who was it against?

188. When did the Glazers complete their takeover of Man Utd?

189. On 17th August 1996 David Beckham scored a goal from the halfway line against which team?

190. Which Man Utd player won the PFA Player of the Year for 2006/07 and for 2007/08?

191. On 13th May 2007 Middlesbrough played the youngest player ever to play PL. Who was it and how old was he?

192. Which Middlesbrough player has received a joint record 3 red cards in a season?

193. Who is the leading PL goal scorer for Middlesbrough?

194. Why was the Blackburn Middlesbrough game of 21st December 1995 exceptional?

195. When did Middlesbrough move from Ayresome Park to the Riverside Stadium?

196. How many seasons have Middlesbrough been in the PL?

197. Who was there top scorer during the inaugural PL season 1992/93?

198. Who was the player signed from Juventus in 1996 for £7m?

199. What was his nickname?

200. Despite relegation in 1996/97 the former Juventus player was still the league's top goal scorer. How many did he score?

201. Which Newcastle player holds the joint record for the number of PL goals in a season and which season?

202. Which Newcastle player holds the joint record of 14 yellow cards in a season?

203. Which Newcastle player has received a joint record 3 red cards in a season?

204. Which player won the golden boot playing for Newcastle in 1993/94?

205. Who is the leading PL goal scorer for Newcastle?

206. In 1993/94 Newcastle achieved the joint highest position by a promoted club. What position did they finish in?

207. Which eight players have scored more than 30 Premier League Goals for Newcastle United?

208. Which retail billionaire became owner of Newcastle United in 2007?

209. In 2005, which two Newcastle United teammates were sent off for fighting against each other in United's Premiership match with Aston Villa?

210. How many times have Newcastle been PL runners up?

211. On August 25th, 1998 Sunderland beat Newcastle 2-1. The Newcastle manager made the headlines though. Why?

212. What year was Kevin Keegan's 'I would love it' rant?

213. How much did Newcastle pay for Alan Shearer?

214. How many seasons have Norwich been in the PL?

215. Who is the leading PL goal scorer for Norwich?

216. In 1992/93 Norwich finished 3rd in the PL. What was their goal difference?

217. What is Norwich's Ground called?

218. What is Norwich's nickname?

219. Which former Chancellor of the Exchequer was appointed Chairman in 2015?

220. On the 6th February 1999 Notts Forest suffered the biggest home defeat in PL history. What was the score and who was it against?

221. Who is the leading PL goal scorer for Notts Forest?

222. In 1994/95 Forest achieved the joint highest position by a promoted club. What position did they finish in?

223. Notts Forest were founder member of the Premier League in 1992/93. What position did they finish?

224. What is Notts Forest's best Premier League finish?

225. Who was their top goal scorer in that season?

226. Who is the leading PL goal scorer for Oldham?

227. How many seasons were Oldham in the PL?

228. Who has made the most PL appearances for Oldham?

229. What is Oldham's ground called?

230. What is Oldham's nickname?

231. On the 29th September 2007 Portsmouth won a game with the highest aggregate score in PL history. Who was it against and what was the score?

232. Who is the leading PL goal scorer for Portsmouth?

233. Who scored the first PL hat trick for Portsmouth?

234. What is the Portsmouth ground called?

235. On the 26th February 2010 Portsmouth did something no other PL club has done. What was it?

236. Who is the leading PL goal scorer for QPR?

237. What is QPR's ground called?

238. When was QPR's last season in the Premier League?

239. Who was their leading goal scorer that season?

240. What was QPR's highest finishing position in the Premier League?

241. Who is the leading PL goal scorer for Reading?

242. Which Reading player was sent off without touching the ball?

243. Reading have spent 3 seasons in the Premier League. What was their highest finishing position?

244. Who was their manager?

245. Which Sheff Utd player scored the first Premier League goal?

246. Who is the leading Premier League goal scorer for Sheff Utd?

247. Which Sheff Utd player was sent off without touching the ball?

248. Who is the leading PL goal scorer for Sheff Weds?

249. Which Sheffield Weds player won the Football Writers player of the year in the inaugural PL season?

250. On 26th September 1995 Sheffield Weds beat Arsenal 1-0. The game was overshadowed by a sending off of a Sheffield Wednesday player. Who was sent off and why?

251. Which Southampton player has scored the fastest PL hat trick and how long did it take?

252. Which Southampton player has the joint record of 14 yellow cards in a season?

253. Which Southampton player has received a joint record 3 red cards in a season?

254. Who is the leading PL goal scorer for Southampton?

255. Two different Argentinian coaches have taken charge of Southampton with the initials 'MP'. Can you name them?

256. Which Southampton manager was the worlds first £2million player?

257. On 23rd November 1996 Southampton played 'George Weah's cousin' who had been signed based on misinformation. Who was the manager who was taken in?

258. On the 26th October 1995 Southampton beat Man Utd. What was the remarkable score?

259. Who was the forward that Southampton sold to Blackburn Rovers in July 1992?

260. Who saved Matt Le Tissier's one penalty miss in 1993?

261. What is Stoke's nickname?

262. In 2014/15 Stoke had their biggest Premier League win of 6-1. Who was it against?

263. In 2017/18 Stoke were relegated. Who was their leading goal scorer that season?

264. What was their largest defeat in the 2017/18 season?

265. How many seasons have Stoke spent in the Premier League?

266. Which Sunderland player holds the record for the most Premier League goals in their debut season?

267. In 2002/03 Sunderland created a PL record for the most consecutive defeats. How many?

268. Which Sunderland player holds the joint record of 14 yellow cards in a season?

269. Who is the leading PL goal scorer for Sunderland?

270. Sunderland holds the joint record for the most losses in a PL season. How many?

271. On October 17th 2009 Sunderland beat Liverpool 1-0 at the Stadium of Light with the most remarkable goal in PL history. What happened?

272. When did Sunderland move from Roker Park to the Stadium of Light?

273. What is Sunderland's nickname?

274. What year did Sunderland achieve their highest PL finish?

275. Who is the leading PL goal scorer for Swansea?

276. Swansea had the only Premier League manager in history to be born in Denmark. Who is he?

277. What is Swansea's ground called?

278. Swansea were promoted from the Championship in the 2010/11 season. Who did they beat in the play off to secure promotion?

279. Who was the manager that took them to the PL?

280. Who was their leading PL scorer in 2011/12, their first PL season?

281. What is Swansea's highest PL finish and what season?

282. Who was their manager during this season?

283. In 1993/94 Swindon conceded a record number of league goals in a PL season. How many?

284. Who is the leading PL goal scorer for Swindon?

285. What is Swindon's nickname?

286. What is their ground called?

287. How many seasons have Swindon been in the Premier League?

288. Tottenham have the highest attendance for a single PL match. Who was it against and how many?

289. Which Spurs player has scored the most PL goals in a calendar year and how many?

290. Which Tottenham player scored a record 5 goals in the first half of a PL game?

291. Who is the leading PL goal scorer for Tottenham?

292. How many changes of manager have Tottenham had during their time in the PL?

293. Which Spurs player scored the fastest goal in PL history?

294. Who transferred from Spurs to Arsenal in 2001?

295. What was Darren Anderton's nickname?

296. In what year was Harry Redknapp appointed manager?

297. Tottenham drew 0-0 in their very first PL game. Who was it against?

298. Who was the world cup winner who won the Spurs player of the year in 1994/95?

299. Who was the manager before Mauricio Pochettino?

300. Which Spurs player won the PFA Player of the Year for 1998/99?

301. Which Spurs player won the PFA Player of the Year for 2010/11 and for 2012/13?

302. Which Watford player holds the joint record of 14 yellow cards in a season?

303. Who is the leading PL goal scorer for Watford?

304. Which three players won full England Caps while with Watford FC?

305. The 1999/00 season was Watford's first in the PL. Who was their manager?

306. Who was their top scorer that year and how many goals did he get?

307. What is the Watford ground called?

308. Who did Watford sign Andre Gray from on the 9th August 2017?

309. Who did Watford sign on loan from Barcelona on 29th January 2018?

310. What geographical record does the Hawthorns ground hold?

311. In 2004/05 West Brom achieved the fewest number of points for a team that avoided relegation. How many points did they get?

312. Which former West Brom player has scored a hat trick in the PL, Championship, League 1, League 2, the FA Cup, the League Cup and his country?

313. On the 19th May 2013 the West Brom home game resulted in the highest scoring draw in PL history. What was the score and who was it against?

314. Who is the leading PL goal scorer for West Brom?

315. Who scored the first PL hat trick for West Brom?

316. On the 26th December 2006 a West Ham player scored a goal against Portsmouth and became the oldest player to ever score a PL goal. Who was he and how old was he?

317. Who is the leading PL goal scorer for West Ham?

318. Which player and subsequently manager of West Ham holds the record for the most games played or managed at one club in the British Leagues?

319. What is their controversial new stadium called?

320. What is their nickname?

321. Who is the leading PL goal scorer for Wigan?

322. Which Wigan player was sent off without touching the ball?

323. What is Wigan's stadium called?

324. What is Wigan's highest Premier League position?

325. Wimbledon hold the record for the lowest average gate over a PL season. What was the average attendance?

326. Which Wimbledon player has received a joint record 3 red cards in a season?

327. Who is the leading PL goal scorer for Wimbledon?

328. What was the nickname used by the media to describe the Wimbledon team of the 1980s and 90s?

329. How many seasons have Wolves been in the Premier League?

330. What is Wolves ground called?

PREMIER LEAGUE QUIZ ANSWERS

1. It was founded on the 20ᵗʰ February 1992, and the first games on August 15ᵗʰ, 1992.

2. 22

3. Manchester United

4. Alan Shearer (Blackburn Rovers & Newcastle United; 1992/93 - 2005/06)

5. 227 goals

6. Arsenal, Chelsea, Everton, Liverpool, Man Utd and Tottenham

7. 310 - Brad Friedel (Blackburn Rovers, Aston Villa & Tottenham Hotspur; 14 August 2004 - 7 October 2012)

8. 8 - Marcus Bent (Crystal Palace, Blackburn Rovers, Ipswich Town, Leicester City, Everton, Charlton Athletic, Wigan Athletic & Wolverhampton Wanderers; 1997/98 - 2010/11)

9. Emirates Stadium

10. Alan Shearer (Blackburn Rovers & Newcastle United; 1992/93 - 2005/06) 11 hat tricks

11. Andrew Cole (Manchester United v Ipswich Town; 4 March 1995), Alan Shearer (Newcastle United v Sheffield Wednesday; 19

September 1999), Jermain Defoe (Tottenham Hotspur v Wigan Athletic; 22 November 2009), Dimitar Berbatov (Manchester United v Blackburn Rovers; 27 November 2010), Sergio Aguero (Manchester City v Newcastle United; 03 October 2015)

12. Sam Allardyce has managed 7 clubs

13. Thirteen

14. Craig Bellamy - Coventry, Newcastle, Blackburn, Liverpool, West Ham, Man City and Cardiff

15. Six. They were Arsenal, Chelsea, QPR, Tottenham, Wimbledon and Crystal Palace

16. Carling

17. Manchester United

18. Swindon

19. Crystal Palace

20. Manchester United

21. Thierry Henri

22. Wimbledon

23. Coventry City

24. 150

25. Ole Gunnar Solskjaer

26. Riyad Mahrez in 2015/16

27. Man City 32 in 2017/18

28. Goals scored

29. Liberty Stadium, Swansea

30. 1996

31. 2003/04

32. Manchester United beat them 2 -0 in October 2004

33. George Graham

34. Eddie How

35. 20

36. 2010/11

37. Trinidad and Tobago

38. Peter Schmeichel against Everton on the 20th October 2001

39. Paul McGrath

40. Australian

41. The Tykes

42. Only once in 1996/97

43. Neal Redfearn (10 goals)

44. 82

45. St Andrews

46. They finished 9th in 2009/10

47. Cameron Jerome

48. Mikael Forssell (29 goals)

49. He is from Finland

50. 1994/95

51. Alan Shearer scored 34 goals in 42 matches

52. Chris Sutton v Leicester

53. 2nd in Division 1 (third tier) in 2017/18

54. £3.6m from Southampton in July 1992

55. The Trotters

56. 13 – In 1995/96, 1997/98 and from 2001/02 to 2011/12

57. 6th in 2004/05

58. Macron Stadium

59. Kevin Davies has scored 67 goals

60. Cherry Bear

61. Vitality Stadium

62. 11,464

63. Burnley

64. Steve Fletcher

65. Two and they are 1999/00 and 2000/01

66. Dean Windass (13 goals)

67. Dean Windass v Derby County 21st April 2000

68. North Commercials Stadium

69. He said he would shave his hair off. They stayed up and he honoured his bet in the centre circle of the first game the following season.

70. Pascal Gross

71. Glenn Murray

72. Falmer Stadium

73. The Seagulls

74. 17 in 2009/10

75. 2013/14 and 2017/18

76. Their first Premier League season was 1997/98

77. Alan Curbishley

78. Roman Abramovich

79. Frank Lampard (147 goals)

80. Jimmy Floyd Hasselbaink (23 goals)

81. 104 goals

82. Cesar Azpilicueta

83. 5 in 2004/05, 2005/06, 2009/10, 2014/15 and 2016/17

84. 9 seasons from 1992/93 to 2000/01

85. Dion Dublin (61 goals)

86. Dion Dublin (18 goals)

87. Peter Ndlovu in August 1992

88. Ricoh Arena

89. Mickey Quinn scored 17 goals

90. 2017/18 they finished 6th in Division 2 (4th tier)

91. 49 points

92. Chris Armstrong (23 goals)

93. 9 in 1992/93, 1994/95, 1997/98, 2004/05 and 2013/14 to 2017/18

94. Selhurst Park

95. Frank de Boer

96. 32 games

97. 20 goals

98. In 2007/08 they had a negative goal difference of 69 goals

99. Dean Sturridge (32 goals)

100. 29 in 2007/08

101. 7 from 1996-97 to 2001/02 and 2007/08

102. 8th in 1998/99

103. Andrei Kanchelskis

104. James Vaughan (Everton v Crystal Palace) 16 years, 270 days

105. Duncan Ferguson

106. Roberto Martinez

107. Martin Keown

108. Mark

109. Craven Cottage

110. Michael Jackson

111. Moritz Volz v Fulham

112. Clint Dempsey (50 goals)

113. Kirklees Stadium

114. The Terriers

115. 2017/18

116. Nikica Jelavic (12 goals)

117. 5 in 2008/09, 2009/2010, 2013/14, 2014/15 and 2016/17

118. He gave his half time talk on the pitch

119. KCOM Stadium

120. Black and amber which gives them their nickname of The Tigers

121. 5 seasons – 1992/93, 1993/94, 1994/95, 2000/01 and 2001/02

122. The score was 9-0 to Manchester United

123. Marcus Stewart (25 goals)

124. Brian Deane v Sheff Utd 16th January 1993

125. 29 in 1994-95

126. Eric Cantona (Leeds United v Tottenham Hotspur; 25 August 1992)

127. Mark Viduka (59 goals)

128. Gordon Strachan v Blackburn 10th April 1993

129. James Milner was 16 years 356 days v Sunderland on Boxing Day 2002

130. Jimmy Floyd Hasselbaink (18 goals)

131. James Vardy (29 August 2015 - 28 November 2015) sored in 11 consecutive games beating Ruud van Nistelrooy's record

132. Robbie Savage in the 2001/02 season

133. Jamie Vardy

134. 24 in 2015/16 as Leicester won the title

135. Wes Morgan in 2015/16

136. 5000/1

137. The King Power Stadium

138. Riyad Mahrez

139. Robbie Fowler (128 goals)

140. Mark Walters v Coventry 17th April 1993

141. Bruce Grobbelaar (1993-94)

142. Luis Suarez (31 goals)

143. 120 goals

144. Roy Evans in 1997

145. Branislov Ivanovic

146. Chelsea

147. Mo Salah

148. Steven Gerrard

149. Zero

150. Chelsea

151. £50m

152. Joe Royle in a dispute over his pay off.

153. The same points as Man Utd but their goal difference was better by 8 goals

154. 10 goals

155. 43 years, 162 days - John Burridge (Manchester City v Queens Park Rangers; 14 May 1995)

156. Sergio Aguerro

157. Nicolas Anelka v Aston Villa 14th September 2003

158. Carlos Tevez (20 goals)

159. It was the earliest ever start of a PL game at 11.15am. It was done to suit the Asian markets.

160. QPR with Man City winning 3-2

161. Sergio Aguero

162. Ederson kicked the ball 75.35m on 10th May 2018 according to the Guinness Book of Records

163. 100 points

164. 106 goals

165. 18 wins

166. 902 passes

167. Wolfsburg

168. Monaco

169. Ryan Giggs – 22 seasons

170. They won by 18 points in 1999/00

171. They have won 13 ((1992/93, 1993/94, 1995/96, 1996/97, 1998/99, 1999/00, 2000/01, 2002/03, 2006/07, 2007/08, 2008/09, 2010/11 & 2012/13)

172. 4 goals

173. 89 points. They were beaten by Man City on goal difference

174. 75 points beating Newcastle into second place

175. 183 - Wayne Rooney (Manchester United; 2004/05 - 2016/17)

176. Ryan Giggs (Manchester United; 1992/93 - 2013/14) – 162 assists

177. Edwin van der Sar (Manchester United; 15 November 2008 - 18 February 2009) – 14 games

178. 13 – (1992/93, 1993/94, 1995/96, 1996/97, 1998/99, 1999/00, 2000/01, 2002/03, 2006/07, 2007/08, 2008/09, 2010/11 & 2012/13)

179. 27 – (August 1993, October 1994, February 1996, March 1996, February 1997, October 1997, January 1999, April 1999, August 1999, March 2000, April 2000, February 2001, April 2003, December 2003, February 2005, March 2006, August 2006, October 2006, February 2007, January 2008, March 2008, January 2009, April 2009, September 2009, January 2011, August 2011, October 2012)

180. 410

181. Ruud van Nistelrooy (25 goals)

182. 109 goals

183. Robert Joseph

184. Andy Cole v Ipswich 4th March 1995

185. Gary Pallister

186. It was at Crystal Palace on the 25th January 1995

187. Man City

188. May 2005

189. Wimbledon

190. Cristiano Ronaldo

191. Matthew Briggs (Middlesbrough v Fulham; 13 May 2007) - 16 years, 68 days

192. Franck Queudrue in the 2002/03 season

193. Hamilton Ricard (31 goals)

194. Because it didn't happen because Middlesbrough claimed they couldn't raise a team because of illness and injury. Middlesbrough were docked 3 points for non-fulfilment of fixture and were relegated by 2 points that season.

195. 1995

196. 15 – 1992/93, 1995/96, 1996/97, 1998-99-2008-09 and 2016/17

197. Paul Wilkinson (15 goals)

198. Fabrizio Ravanelli

199. The White Feather in reference to his hair

200. 31

201. Andrew Cole in 1993/94 scored 34 in 42 matches

202. Cheick Tiote in the 2010/11 season

203. David Batty in the 1997/98 season

204. Andy Cole (34 goals)

205. Alan Shearer (148 goals)

206. 3rd 1993-94

207. Alan Shearer (148 goals), Peter Beardsley (47), Shola Ameobi (43), Andrew Cole (43), Les Ferdinand (41), Papiss Cissé (37), Nolberto Solano (37) and Rob Lee (34)

208. Mike Ashley the owner of Sports Direct

209. Lee Bowyer and Kieron Dyer

210. Twice in 1995/96 and 1996/97 both times to Man Utd

211. Ruud Gullit dropped Alan Shearer and Duncan Ferguson

212. 29th April 1996

213. £15m

214. 8 – 1992/93, 1993/94, 1994/95, 2004/05, 2011/12, 2012/13 and 2015/16

215. Chris Sutton (33 goals)

216. Surprisingly it was -4

217. Carrow Road

218. The Canaries

219. Ed Balls

220. 1-8 Notts Forest v Man Utd

221. Bryan Roy (24 goals)

222. 3rd 1994/95

223. 22nd

224. They finished 3rd in 1994/95

225. Stan Collymore scored 25 goals

226. Graham Sharp (16 goals)

227. Two seasons -1992/93 and 1993/94

228. Mike Milligan (81 appearances)

229. Boundary Park

230. The Latics

231. 7-4 Portsmouth v Reading

232. Aiyegbeni Yakubu (29 goals)

233. Teddy Sheringham v Bolton 26th August 2003

234. Fratton Park

235. They went into administration while in the PL.

236. Les Ferdinand (61 goals)

237. Loftus Road

238. 2014/15

239. Charlie Austin

240. They finished 5th in the inaugural year of 1992/93

241. Kevin Doyle (19 goals)

242. Dave Kitson in the 2007/08 game against Man Utd. He was on the pitch for 37 seconds after coming off the bench

243. They finished 8th in 2006/07

244. Steve Coppell

245. Brian Deane (Sheffield United v Manchester United - 15 August 1992)

246. Brian Deane again (15 goals)

247. Keith Gillespie against Reading in 2006/07. He was sent off 15 seconds after coming off the bench

248. Mark Bright (48 goals)

249. Chris Waddle

250. Paolo di Canio was sent off for pushing the referee over.

251. Sadio Mane (Southampton v Aston Villa; 16 May 2015) 2 minutes, 56 seconds

252. Mark Hughes in the 1998/99 season

253. Victor Wanyama in the 2015/16 season

254. Matt Le Tissier (101 goals)

255. Mauricio Pochettino & Mauricio Pellegrino

256. Mark Hughes

257. Graham Souness

258. 6-3

259. Alan Shearer

260. Mark Crossley

261. The Potters

262. Liverpool

263. Xherdan Shaqiri

264. It was a 7-2 defeat to Manchester City

265. 10 seasons from 2008/09 till relegation in 2017/18

266. Kevin Phillips in 1999-2000

267. 15

268. Lee Cattermole in the 2014/15 season

269. Kevin Phillips (61 goals)

270. 29 in 2005-06

271. The ball deflected off a beach ball

272. 1997

273. The Black Cats

274. They finished 7th in 1999/00 and 2000/01

275. Gylfi Sigurdsson (34 goals)

276. Michael Laudrup on the 15th June 2012

277. Liberty Stadium

278. Reading

279. Brendan Rogers

280. Danny Graham

281. 8th in 2014/15

282. Gary Monk

283. 100 goals

284. Jan-Aage Fjortoft (12 goals)

285. The Robins

286. County Ground

287. One season 1993/94

288. 83,222 against Arsenal at Wembley on 10th February 2018

289. Harry Kane in 2017 scored 39 PL goals

290. Jermain Defoe (Tottenham Hotspur v Wigan Athletic; 22 November 2009)

291. Harry Kane

292. 21

293. Ledley King. His first goal for Tottenham Hotspur (v. Bradford City) came just 10 seconds into the game on 9th December 2000.

294. Sol Campbell

295. Sicknote, somewhat cruelly due to the amount of time he was injured

296. October 2008

297. Southampton

298. Jurgen Klinsmann

299. Tim Sherwood

300. David Ginnola

301. Gareth Bale

302. Jose Holebas in the 2016/17 season

303. Troy Deeney

304. John Barnes, Luther Blissett and Ben Foster

305. Graham Taylor

306. Heioar Helguson scored 6 goals

307. Vicarage Road

308. Burnley

309. Gerard Deulofeu

310. It is the highest above sea level of any ground in the country at 552 feet above sea level

311. 34 points

312. Robbie Earnshaw

313. 5-5 West Brom v Man Utd

314. Peter Odemwingie (30 goals)

315. Robert Earnshaw v Charlton 19th March 2005

316. Teddy Sheringham 40 years, 268 days

317. Paolo di Canio (48 goals)

318. Billy Bonds

319. The Olympic Stadium

320. The Hammers

321. Will Grigg

322. Andreas Johansson in 2005/06 against Arsenal. He came on as a substitute, gave away a penalty and got sent off without touching the ball.

323. DW Stadium

324. 10th in their first Premier League season of 2005/06

325. During the 1992/93 season Wimbledon had an average gate of 8,353 at Selhurst Park

326. Vinnie Jones in the 1995/96 season

327. Dean Holdsworth (58 goals)

328. The Crazy Gang

329. They have had 5 seasons – 2003/04, 2009/10, 2010/11, 2011/12 and 2018/19

330. Molyneux

Made in the USA
Las Vegas, NV
05 December 2022

61226731R00059